PLANET EARTH, 

NATURE

&

FREE ENERGY

INFOMATION BOOK BY

A. SHAW

Planet Earth, Nature & Free Energy.

Introduction

Chapter 1: Our Global Climate

Chapter 2: What Is Causing Climate Change?

Chapter 3: Nature Feeling The Squeeze

Chapter 4: Mass Extinction

Chapter 5: What Does The Future Hold?

Chapter 6: Making Change

Chapter 7: History Of Free Energy

Chapter 8: Different Types Of Alternative Energy

Chapter 9: Methods On Being Renewable From Home

Chapter 10: It's Not All Doom & Gloom

Conclusion

INTRODUCTION

Free energy has the benefit that it can be saved, it doesn't hurt or contaminate the climate, it is produced normally and persistently recharged. The acknowledged sub-arrangement of free fuel sources incorporate sun based, bio-fuels, wind energy, biomass digester, geothermal, hydro e.t.c.

The biomass alternative is subject to biodegradable waste which can be attained from living things or dead creatures. The biomass alternative has less green house impact on the earth's surface than a non-renewable energy source.

The incorporation of the free energy as an elective energy and might be suitable relying upon its source. Nonetheless, the free energy choice has been smothered and not considered by particular nations. It is accepted that free energy concealment is connected to government & corporation interference. Subsequently, free energy choice has not been believed to be innovatively suitable, contamination free, and at no-cost.

In this exploration it will be suggested that free energy can possibly fulfil energy needs, not just in the under developed nations but also for the current global power houses.

Chapter 1
Our Global Climate

CHAPTER 1: OUR GLOBAL CLIMATE.

Human tension on nature has taken off since the 1970s. We have been utilizing an ever increasing number of natural resources, and this has included some major disadvantages.
Quite bluntly we are losing enormous segments of the regular world, human quality of life will be severely reduced and the lives of future generations will be Threatened unless effective action is taken.

In the course of 50 years, nature's ability to help us has plummeted, Air and water quality are diminishing, soils are draining, crops are shy of pollinators, and coasts are less shielded from storms.

Chapter 2

What Is Causing
Climate Change?

CHAPTER 2: WHAT IS CAUSING CLIMATE CHANGE?

In the measure of time it took you to peruse to this point on this page from the last page three waste vehicles worth of plastic have been added to the world's seas, as stipulated previously. There are a large number of square miles of trash dirtying the seas.

contamination incorporates microplastics—plastic trash under five millimetres (0.2 inch) long. Their little size makes these pieces especially guileful, as they are probably going to be confused with food or ingested incidentally by marine life. Microplastics are presently unavoidable, having been distinguished in huge numbers in both ocean water and new water, in airborne residue, in landfills, in apparel, beautifying agents, and regular family items, in human food and drinking water, and in the tissues and stomach related parcels of an incredible assortment of marine and earthbound creatures, including people. The drawn out impacts of microplastics on living frameworks and the climate are obscure. The seas are additionally dirtied with "apparition" fishing gear—comprising of lost or disposed of fishing hardware, including gill nets—

that currently frequents the water by proceeding to catch and slaughter marine life.

Different types of contamination are the outcome of expanded industrialization and urbanization since the twentieth century and moderately ongoing innovative turns of events. We presently fight with commotion contamination and light contamination, poisonous (substance) squander dumps, and electronic waste. Reusing offices, where they exist, can be overpowered by the volume of recyclables or by the assortment of their parts. There are currently a great many sorts of normal plastics, and not every one of them are recyclable. Perhaps the most well-known sorts, polystyrene (otherwise called Styrofoam), is regularly not acknowledged for reusing. It's up to us as buyers to comprehend what is and isn't recyclable locally and to discover suitable offices.

CHAPTER 3
NATURE FEELING THE SQUEEZE

CHAPTER 3: NATURE FEELING THE SQUEEZE

Since the 1970s, Earth's populace has multiplied, The world is progressively overseen in a manner that amplifies the progression of material from nature, to satisfy rising human needs for assets like food, energy and wood.

Subsequently, people have straightforwardly changed at any rate 70% of Earth's territory, essentially for developing plants and keeping creatures. These exercises require deforestation, the corruption of land, loss of biodiversity and contamination, and they affect land and freshwater environments.

About 77% of waterways longer than 1,000 kilometres at this point don't stream openly from source to the ocean, regardless of supporting huge number of individuals.

The fundamental driver of sea change is overfishing, however 66% of the sea's surface has likewise been influenced by different cycles like spillover from farming and plastic contamination.

Live coral cover on reefs has almost split in the previous 150 years and is anticipated to vanish totally inside the following 80 years.

Coral reefs are home to the absolute most assorted biological systems on earth. The quantity of outsider species - species discovered external their normal reach -
has ascended, as people move organic entities all throughout the planet, which upsets and regularly lessens the wealth of nearby biodiversity. This, joined with huma n-driven changes in territory, additionally compromises numerous endemic species.
Furthermore, less assortments of plants and animals are being safeguarded because of standardisations in cultivating rehearses, market inclinations, huge scope exchange and loss of neighbourhood and native information.
Nature additionally benefits people in non-material manners. We gain from it and are motivated by it. It gives us physical and mental encounters and supports our character and feeling of spot. Yet, its ability to offer these types of assistance has likewise decreased.
The deficiency of biological systems is caused principally by changes in land and ocean use, abuse, environmental change, contamination and the presentation of obtrusive species. A few things straightforwardly affect nature, similar to the unloading of waste into the sea.
Huge territories of land oversaw by Indigenous Peoples are encountering a decrease in environments at a more slow rate than wherever else. However, the privileges of Indigenous Peoples are being compromised, which could bring about quicker disintegration of these zones. This would inconveniently affect more extensive environments and social orders.
Exchanging abroad has expanded by 900% since the beginning of the post-modern time and the extraction of living materials from nature has ascended by 200%.
The developing actual distance among organic market implies individuals don't see the annihilation brought about by their utilization.
Japan, US and Europe alone devoured 64% of the world's imports

of fish items.

Big time salary nations have their own fisheries however the majority of these have imploded. Fishing currently happens in unexploited or underexploited fisheries, the majority of which have a place with low-pay nations.

Human effects on the common habitat are presently extraordinary to such an extent that we are dissolving our own economies and food security, as indicated by the world's driving environmental researchers.

Each biological system all throughout the planet is influenced by elimination, from coral reefs to tropical wildernesses, and the issue is speeding up as time passes.

It is assessed that around 1,000,000 creatures and plants are compromised with termination - like never before in mankind's set of experiences. Over 40% of land and water proficient species, about 33% of reef-framing corals and in excess of 33% of all marine warm blooded animals are undermined.

Also, it is humankind that is at fault, as about 75% of conditions ashore have been altogether changed by human activities, in addition to generally 66% of the marine climate.

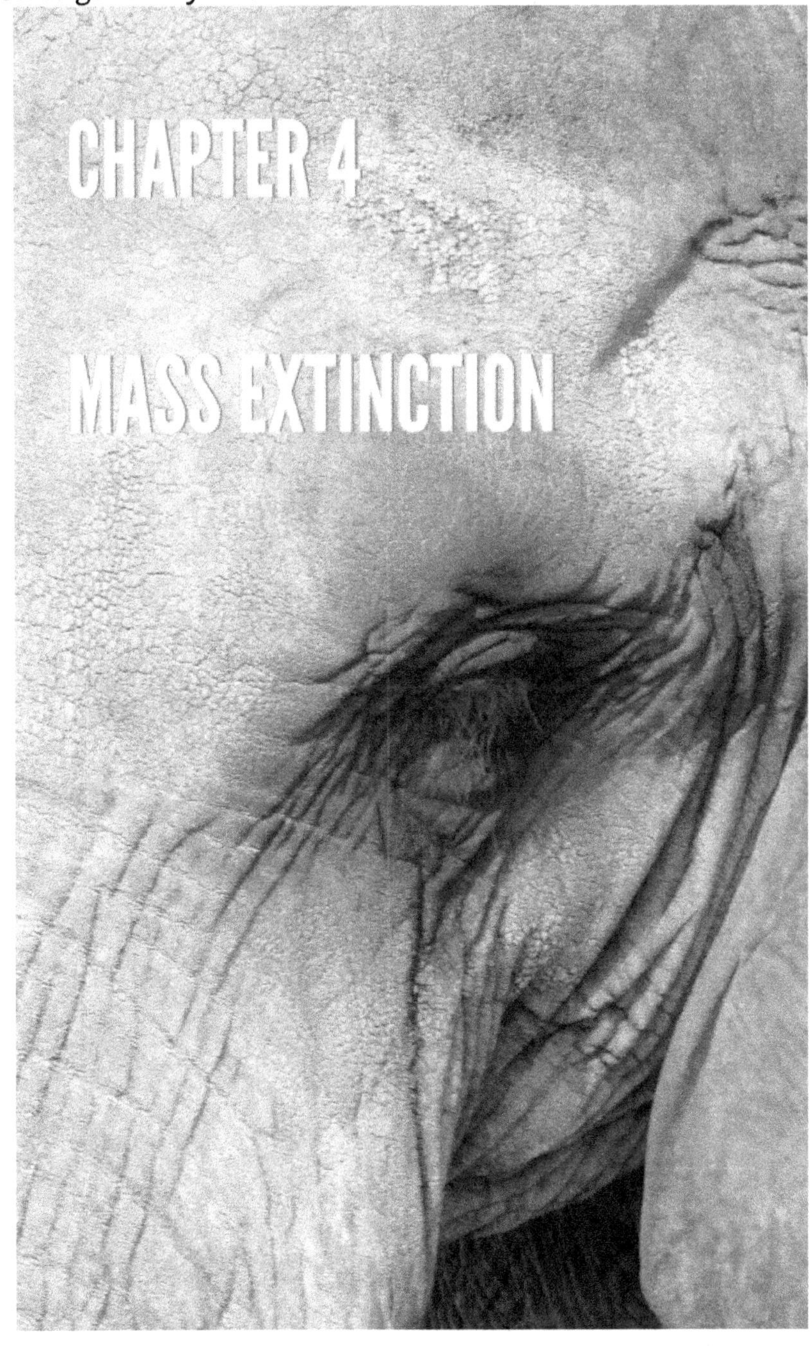

CHAPTER 4: MASS EXTINCTION

The 6th mass termination of wildlife on Earth is speeding up, as per an examination by researchers who caution it could be a tipping point for the breakdown of civilisation.

In excess of 500 types of land creatures were discovered to be near the precarious edge of eradication and liable to be lost inside 20 years. In correlation, a similar number were lost over the entire of the most recent century. Without the human obliteration of nature, even this pace of misfortune would have required millennia, the researchers said.

The land vertebrates very nearly termination, with less than 1,000 left, incorporate the Sumatran rhino, the Clarión wren, the Española giant turtle and the harlequin frog. Notable information was accessible for 77% of the species and the researchers found these had lost 94% of their populaces.

The analysts likewise cautioned of a cascading type of influence, with the deficiency of one animal groups tipping others that rely upon it over the edge.

"Termination breeds eliminations," they said, noticing that dissimilar to other ecological issues annihilation is irreversible.

Mankind depends on biodiversity for its well-being and prosperity, researchers said, with the Covid pandemic a limit illustration of the perils of desolating the regular world. Rising human populace, annihilation of natural surroundings, the untamed life exchange, contamination and the environment emergency should all be critically handled.

Chapter 5

What does the
future hold?

CHAPTER 5:
WHAT DOES THE
FUTURE HOLD?

A report examined in detail how the world will look under three totally different situations.

Worldwide manageability: the entire world movements towards maintainability by regarding ecological limits and ensuring financial advancement incorporates everybody. Abundance is disseminated equally, assets and energy are utilized less, and accentuation is on financial development and human prosperity.

Local rivalry: there is an ascent in patriotism with the attention for the most part on home-grown issues. There is less interest in schooling, especially in the creating sc

ene. Top level salary nations will keep sending out the harm, bringing about some solid and enduring ecological obliteration for people in the future to manage.

Financial hopefulness: the world places confidence in new and imaginative advancements that are still to be concocted, which help us adapt to natural issues.

Emanations will proceed, however with the possibility that innovation will alleviate them. There will be more grounded interest in well-being and schooling, and worldwide business sectors are sensibly incorporated with shared objectives.

Planet Earth, Nature & Free Energy.
Battling the deficiency of biological systems will be mind bog-

gling and will require a nexus approach. This implies contemplating how various segments of the issue like nature, legislative issues and economics all interface with each other.

An illustration of a nexus approach is decrease biodiversity misfortune by changing how we ranch, while simultaneously ensuring individuals have sufficient food, their occupations are not subverted, and social clashes are not disturbed.

The best approach to keep away from a portion of these issues might be to zero in on recovering and re-establishing high-carbon environments like woodlands and wetlands. Essentially the requirement for food could be met by changing dietary decisions and lessening waste.

Changing to clean energy is a significant advance which would permit different changes to happen all the more without any problem. Acquiring coal and gas includes annihilating tremendous measures of land and seascapes just as contaminating the climate past extraction.

Planet Earth, Nature & Free Energy.

Be that as it may, to accomplish this completely, the world requirements to revaluate current political designs and cultural standards, which tend not to look after nature. One method of doing that is by improving existing natural approaches and guidelines, just as eliminating and changing destructive strategies.

CHAPTER 6: MAKING CHANGES

We're on this planet and in this battle together.

We as a general public made this wreck, and it's greater than any of us, or even any 1,000,000 of us. We need to meet up to switch the harm we've dispensed on our planet. Little advances matter. Possibly they matter significantly more than you know at the present time. Acting with moral duty toward the climate is a strong initial step, and we trust that you learn something here that will engage you to make life changes that emphatically sway the climate. We likewise need to look for equity for the climate on a greater scale by requesting that our policymakers focus on the conservation and enhancement of the climate, the insurance of imperilled species, and the manageable utilization of common assets.

We know the issues that we have illustrated here are desperate, yet it is with an inclination of confidence that we present Saving Earth.

The difficulties confronting humankind are extraordinary, and it isn't for some esteem that we say that catastrophe is approaching. Yet, with information and comprehension and responsibility—and expectation—those difficulties can be survived and the planet safeguarded for people in the future.

CHAPTER 7

HISTORY OF FREE ENERGY

CHAPTER 7: HISTORY OF FREE ENERGY

There are some unsourced claims that an interminable movement machine called the "sorcery wheel" (a wheel turning on its hub controlled by lodestones) showed up in eighth century Bavaria. This authentic case gives off an impression of being unconfirmed however regularly rehashed.

Early plans of never-ending movement machines were finished by Indian mathematician–cosmologist Bhaskara II, who portrayed a wheel (Bhāskara's wheel) that he asserted would run forever.

A drawing of an unending movement machine showed up in the sketchbook of Villard de Honnecourt, a thirteenth century French expert artisan and designer. The sketchbook was worried about mechanics and design.

Following the case of Villard, Peter of Maricourt planned an attractive globe which, in the event that it were mounted without erosion corresponding to the divine hub, would pivot once per day. It was proposed to fill in as a programmed armillary sphere.

Leonardo da Vinci made various drawings of gadgets he trusted would make free energy. Leonardo da Vinci was for the most part against such gadgets, however drew and analysed various overbalanced wheels.

Nikolai Tesla

Tesla is the notable brand name of business person expert Elon Musk and his electric vehicles, yet what might be said about Tesla, the man?

Over 100 years prior, Nikola Tesla (1856-1943) developed substituting current (AC), the polyphase rotating current framework, which established the framework for the present mass-delivered power supply.

From the creation of the molecule bar to radar, the electric vehicle, advanced mechanics, and far off controlled robots, Tesla mental-demonstrated answers for issues with such lucidity of psyche that he could imagine the individual pieces of a machine or instrument in three measurements. At that point run re-enactments in his mind and check for mileage.

He even spearheaded interplanetary radio correspondence with Guglielmo Marconi. Whom he later dropped out with when the US Patent Office bafflingly upset his licenses and adequately acknowledged Marconi for the innovation of the radio; who was, indeed, utilizing a few of Tesla's licenses.

Tesla was so a long ways relatively radical, the virtuoso of a significant number of his initial innovations — used to build up the radio and TV, fluorescent and acceptance lighting, and MRIs and X-beams – - just became known after his passing.

Tesla's for some time held dream was to make a wellspring of unlimited, clean energy that was free for everybody. He unequivocally went against concentrated coal-terminated force stations that heaved carbon dioxide into the air that people relaxed.

He accepted that the Earth had "liquid electrical charges" running underneath its surface, that when hindered by a progression of electrical releases at rehashed set spans, would create a boundless force supply by producing tremendous low-recurrence electrical waves.

One of Tesla's most uncommon investigations was to communicate electrical control over significant distances without wires or links was an accomplishment that has confounded researchers from that point onward.His fantastic vision was to liberate humanity from the weights of separating, siphoning, moving, and consuming petroleum derivatives, which he saw as "corrupt waste".

The present petroleum derivative industry, a tradition of that past, has battled similarly as hard in late a very long time to secure similar interests — Luddites and slow pokes scared of losing their organizations to the breeze and the sun.

Chapter 8

Different Types
Of Alternative
Energy

CHAPTER 8: DIFFERENT TYPES OF ALTERNATIVE ENERGY

Hydrogen Gas

In contrast to different types of gaseous petrol, hydrogen is a totally spotless consuming fuel. Once created, hydrogen gas cells radiate possibly water fume and warm air when being used.

The significant issue with this type of elective energy is that it is for the most part gotten from the utilization of flammable gas and petroleum products.

Thusly, it very well may be contended that the discharges made to extricate it neutralize the advantages of its utilization.

The cycle of electrolysis, which is fundamental for the parting of water into hydrogen and oxygen, makes this less of an issue. Notwithstanding, electrolysis actually positions underneath the recently referenced strategies for getting hydrogen, however research keeps on making it more proficient and financially savvy.

Flowing Energy

While flowing energy utilizes the force of water to produce energy, similar as with hydroelectric strategies, its application really shares more for all intents and purpose with wind turbines much of the time.

Despite the fact that it is a genuinely new innovation, its latent capacity is gigantic. A report delivered in the United Kingdom assessed that flowing energy could meet however much 20% of the UK's flow power requests.

The most well-known type of flowing energy age is the utilization of Tidal Stream Generators. These utilization the active energy of the sea to control turbines, without delivering the misuse of petroleum derivatives or being as defenceless to the components as different types of elective energy.

Biomass Energy

Biomass energy arrives in various structures. Consuming wood has been utilized for millennia to make heat, however later headways have additionally seen squander, like that in landfills, and liquor items utilized for comparable purposes.

Zeroing in on consuming wood, the warmth produced can be identical to that of a warming framework. Moreover, the costs included will in general be lower and the measure of carbon delivered by this sort of fuel falls beneath the sum delivered by non-renewable energy sources.

There are various issues that you need to consider with these frameworks, particularly whenever introduced in the home. Upkeep can be a factor, in addition to you may have to obtain authorization from a nearby position to Introduce one.

Wind Energy

This type of energy age has gotten progressively mainstream lately. It offers a lot of the very advantages that numerous other elective fuel sources do in that it utilizes a sustainable source and produces no waste.

Current breeze energy establishments power approximately twenty million homes in the United States each year and that number is developing. Most states in the country presently have some type of wind energy set-up and interest into the innovation keeps on developing.

Shockingly, this type of energy age additionally presents difficulties. Wind turbines confine sees and might be perilous to certain types of untamed life.

Geothermal Power

At its generally fundamental, geothermal force is tied in with separating energy from the beginning us. It is becoming progressively famous, with the area overall encountering five percent development in 2015.

The World Bank right now gauges that around forty nations could meet the majority of their force requests utilizing geothermal force.

This force source has huge potential while doing little to disturb the land. Be that as it may, the substantial forthright expenses of making geothermal force plants has prompted more slow reception than may have been normal for a fuel source with such a lot of guarantee.

Flammable gas

Flammable gas sources have been being used for various many years, however it is through the movement of pressure proced-ures that it is turning into a more suitable elective fuel source. Specifically, it is being utilized in vehicles to diminish fossil fuel byproducts.
Interest for this fuel source has been expanding. In 2016, the lower 48
conditions of the United States arrived at record levels of interest and utilization.
The potential for pollution is bigger than with other elective fuel sources and flammable gas actually emanates ozone depleting substances, regardless of whether the sum is lower than with pet-roleum derivatives.

Biofuels

As opposed to biomass fuel sources, biofuels utilize creature and vegetation to make energy. Generally they are powers that can be gotten from some type of natural matter.
They are inexhaustible in situations where plants are utilized, as these can be regrown consistently. Notwithstanding, they do require devoted hardware for extraction, which can add to ex-panded emanations regardless of whether biofuels themselves don't.
Biofuels are progressively being embraced, especially in the United States. They represented around seven percent of trans-port fuel utilization starting at 2012.

Wave Energy

Water again demonstrates itself to be an important supporter of elective fuel sources with wave energy converters. These hold a benefit over flowing fuel sources since they can be put in the sea in different circumstances and areas.

Similar as with flowing energy, the advantages come in the absence of waste created. It is additionally more solid than numerous different types of elective energy and has huge potential when utilized appropriately.

Once more, the expense of such frameworks is a significant contributing element to moderate take-up. We likewise don't yet have sufficient information to discover what wave energy converters mean for normal environments.

Hydroelectric Energy

Hydroelectric strategies really are the absolute most punctual methods for making energy, however their utilization started to decrease with the ascent of petroleum derivatives. Regardless of this, they actually represent around seven percent of the energy delivered in the United States.

Hydroelectric energy conveys with it various advantages. In addition to the fact that it is a spotless wellspring of energy, which implies it doesn't make contamination and the heap gives that emerge from it, yet it is additionally an environmentally friendly power source.

Even better, it likewise offers various optional advantages that are not promptly obvious. The dams utilized in creating hydroelectric force additionally add to flood control and water system strategies.

Atomic Power

Atomic force is among the most bountiful types of elective energy. It makes various direct advantages regarding emanations and proficiency, while additionally boosting the economy by making occupations in plant creation and activity.
Thirteen nations depended on atomic ability to deliver at any rate a fourth of their power starting at 2015 and there are at present 450 plants in activity all through the world.
The downside is that when something turns out badly with a thermal energy station the potential for disaster exists. The circumstances in Chernobyl and Fukushima are instances of this.

Sun based Power

At the point when the vast majority consider elective fuel sources they will in general utilize sun based force for instance. The innovation has developed hugely throughout the long term and is presently utilized for

huge scope energy creation and force age for single homes.
Various nations have acquainted activities with advance the development of sunlight based force. The United Kingdom's 'Feed-

in Tariff' is one model, similar to the United States' 'Sun powered Investment Tax Credit'.

This fuel source is totally inexhaustible and the expenses of establishment are exceeded by the cash saved in energy bills from customary providers. By the by, sun oriented cells are inclined to crumbling throughout enormous time frames and are not as successful in unideal climate conditions.

CHAPTER 9: METHODS ON BEING RENEWABLE FROM HOME

Save water. Don't wash the dishes.

Let them pile up to the point where you're actually wondering if it's ok to eat soup from a dog's bowl. Then, and only then, casually load the dirty pots into a dishwasher. Press the start button. Now sit down and catch your breath.

A fully loaded dishwasher can be more water efficient than washing by hand.

Even if you're using a washing-up bowl.

Help bees. Don't mow the lawn.

Look at your neighbours joyfully murdering the life out of their garden again.

They won't sleep soundly until they've lopped the head off every buttercup, daisy and bee-friendly dandelion.

What would an eco warrior do? Absolutely nothing. Pull up a chair, grab a cocktail and watch the grass grow – you green god.

Leaving even part of your garden t

o grow wild can help pollinating insects, like bees, thrive.

Avoid plastic packaging.

Takeaway food and drink often come in plastic food containers with disposable utensils. They're a big part of the plastic pollution in our waste system. And as we know, disposing of them doesn't mean they disappear. A lot of disposables are landfilled, blown or washed into waterways or end up as yet more plastic pollution in our rivers and oceans.

To encourage a society that reuses instead of throwing away, governments should actualy ban disposable plastic items.

Eat Less Meat.

If you really want to get good at this eco lark, you're going to have to learn to do less – like eating less meat. Yeah that steak might look good, but think how tiring it's going to be to chomp on.

Meat and dairy production is responsible for 14.5% of climate changing gases (more than all forms of transport).

Chewing is work. The clever environmentalist indulges in meat-free food that requires less mouth muscle.

Help the planet with a veg box

If you're keen to avoid supermarkets and after organic, planet-friendly food, then veg box deliveries will be right up your street. Ordering an organic veg box helps keep our pollinators safe from chemicals. It also invites less plastic waste into your home, and can help cut down on separate car journeys – reducing your carbon emissions.

Organic bell peppers in yellow, orange and red.

Plant trees.

No, you don't need to plant anything; Ecosia does.

It's a search engine that plants trees with the money it makes from ads. Every time you click on an ad in your search results, you're helping to reforest the Earth. I like doing this in between streaming videos of people planting trees.

Be aware, if you block adverts, you won't be helping the planet.

Clean the air, Get a cheap ride.

Find a driver going to the same place as you. By sharing a ride with others – or as I like to call it, being driven around by someone – you'll be helping to reduce air pollution.

Support clean energy.
We both know that your talents are better served in a hammock pretending to read a book.
Switch to renewable energy instead. Lie back and watch it happen in as little as 5 minutes. No disruption to your supply and no engineers asking you to make tea.
It's cheaper than you think and means your dreams of an eco-powered robot butler are still well and truly alive.

CHAPTER 10: IT'S NOT ALL DOOM & GLOOM

One examination took a gander at a worldwide temperature alteration, air contamination and energy instability, making Green New Deal guides for 143
nations to defeat these issues stated within this book.

The guides require these nations, which are on the whole liable for 99.7% of worldwide CO2 outflows, to change to 100% perfect, inexhaustible breeze, water and sunlight based force no later than 2050, with at any rate 80% by 2030.

The investigation partitions every one of the planet's nations into 24 districts which can cooperate on network steadiness and energy stockpiling arrangements, so energy request matches supply between 2050 to 2052. From that point forward, it's feasible to control the planet altogether by practical energy.

Changing to wind, water and sun powered worldwide could wipe out 4 to 7million passings from air contamination every year, while first easing back and afterward switching the impacts of an Earth-wide temperature boost and, in doing as such, balancing out the worldwide energy area.

Certainly, challenges exist and the objectives are aspiring. In any case, the reports all presume that the innovation exists for the world to progress to a completely supportable energy framework by 2050, which should keep the planet underneath the 1.5° Paris Agreement a worldwide temperature alteration target.

Conclusion

Conclusion

My conclusion is that the worldwide temperature alteration is a significant test for our worldwide society. There is certainty that our Earth-wide polluting will change our environment even more in the later part of the century. So what are the answers for an unnatural weather change? To begin with, there should be a global political arrangement.

Second, subsidizing for creating modest and clean energy creation should be expanded, as all financial advancement depends on expanding energy utilization. We should not place all our faith on worldwide governmental Issues, rather in clean energy innovation, so we should get ready for the most terrible and adjust. We should be prepared and start making significant change now before a great deal of harm is caused to ourselves and our beautiful planet.

Thank You For Reading,

Disclaimer

The purpose of this ebook is to educate. The author and the publisher do not warrant that the information contained in this ebook is fully complete and shall not be responsible for any errors or omissions. The author and publisher shall have neither liability nor responsibility to any person or entity with respect to any loss or damage caused or alleged to be caused directly or indirectly by this ebook.